"101 Rules of Relationships contains exceptional principles of relationship gleaned from Billy Hornsby's vast experience as a law enforcement officer, missionary and pastor. The book is exceptional because Billy is an exceptional man of uncompromising integrity and places an extremely high value on family and personal relationships.

I recently completed a 24-year career in law enforcement, began a new one in ministry, and along with my wife, am raising our five children. Billy has modeled and taught me excellent principles regarding these important areas of my life. Our children call him "Uncle Billy". Billy is a true mentor to me and I can't wait for the next time we eat hummus together."

Marcus Wright
Associate Pastor
Church of the Highlands
Birmingham, AL

"This book, 101 Rules for Relationships – Relational Intersections, is one that I will give to many of my friends and family. It expresses the issues that are central to long-lasting healthy relationships. Billy is my best friend. I have known and worked with him for many years and can truthfully say that, 'Billy lives these rules!'

Rule number 6 is, "Invest time in our friends." He has invested time in our friendship by having me travel with him around the world and I have seen him do the same for others. Put these principles into practice and you will know what valuable relationships are all about."

Hank Henagan
Associate Pastor
Bethany World Prayer Center
Baker, LA

"This book is a gem. It is chock-full of helpfully enlightening "rules" that will greatly benefit any reader, regardless of age or gender. Billy Hornsby draws from his great wealth of experience as a husband, father, and seasoned minister, who has been privileged with the opportunity of teaching life-changing truths to people around the world.

Much like John Maxwell, Billy Hornsby uses humor and wit to capture his readers' hearts and minds. This book is another example of his unusual ability to integrate truths into the "real-life" situations that each of us experience in our daily life.

I so enjoyed this book, especially its practical nature, that I read it in its entirety in one sitting. I'm sure there are 101 other rules that could have been gathered and printed; these 101 are surely well chosen."

Bill Ollendike

101 Rules for Relationships

101 Relational Intersections

by

Billy Hornsby

VarnerMiller Publishing

Second Edition

Published by VarnerMiller Publishing
Reprinted 2011

Copyright ©2002 by Billy Hornsby

VarnerMiller Publishing
887 Johnnie Dodds BLVD
Suite 130
Mount Pleasant, SC 29464

For information on ordering copies of 101 Rules for
Relationships—Relational Intersections, contact Billy Hornsby at
(205) 981-4566 or visit www.billyhornsby.com.

Printed in the United States of America

ISBN: 0-9721195-0-7

Library of Congress Control Number: 2002107727

Dedication

This book is dedicated to my brothers Frank, Butch, Scott, and Brent, my sister Suzanne, my parents, Sidney and Williamette Hornsby, and my co-workers. To my wife Charlene, my daughters Tammy, Trudy, and Shary, and my sons-in-law Chris, David, and Phil.

To my friends Ronnie Bennett, Joe Bowles, Hank Henagan, Bill Ollendike, Greg Surratt, and Marcus Wright.

To all of you with whom I have such an incredible relationship, and who have made my life very rich... I dedicate this book.

Acknowledgements

For their excellent work on the editing, graphics design, and support in producing this book, I want to thank Lori Miller, Gayle Bennett, Christina Hendricks, Jim Yohn, Dr. Joe Bowles, and Nancy Heinz for making 101 Rules for Relationships-Relational Intersections possible.

Inspiration for this book

Some time ago, before I wrote this book, a dear friend called me to meet him for lunch. We met at a favorite Lebanese restaurant in town and began to chat and discuss old and new "business" as we always do. While waiting for our food, we ordered an appetizer of hummus and pita bread. When we were sharing the dish, I noticed that Marcus would drag his fork through the hummus and eat off it or use it to spread hummus on his bread. He would repeat this double dipping exercise with no regard for the fact that I wanted some too. I was miffed at this. I pushed the saucer of hummus towards him and said, "Go ahead Marcus, you can have the whole thing." I was annoyed that he was so inconsiderate of me and would "poison" the food in that way.

First of all, it struck me that I wasn't mature enough to handle such a small violation. And secondly, that something so minor could cause ripples in a great relationship. Marcus is a dear long time friend. I should not have reacted that way.

A small infraction like "double-dipping" can cause relationships to falter. Though not intentional or serious, it can be perceived in the wrong light and hurt an otherwise great relationship. As I meditated on what happened at the restaurant that day I got the inspiration to write a short book that describes how relationships intersect and how they sometimes crash as a result.

Within a minute we were laughing about it. He apologized and ordered me my own dish of hummus and everything was fine again. Marcus remains one of my dearest friends.

After spending time with someone, he or she will walk away, loving you a little more, or a little less. Life is more enjoyable when they love you a little more.

Enjoy the next few pages, you will find yourself in many of them.

And now, the rules...

Rule 1

Don't take life, or this book, too seriously.

O f course there are things in life that we must take seriously: God, health, family, etc. However, I have noticed that people who are always serious-minded about everything have few friends. They seem to focus on being right about things rather than friendly to others. Their "rightness" often limits their ability to tolerate inconsistencies in another and too often is the reason they don't befriend that person. Anyway, why not just rejoice in the days that God gives us with our friends and loved ones? "A merry heart does good like a medicine." (Proverbs 17:22 -KJV) So what if you or they are not always correct about everything? Get happy, just say, "C'est la vie" (That's life!)

Rule 2

Laissez le bon temps roule.

The State of Louisiana has a great slogan. It means, "Let the good times roll!" Driving through Texas once, I saw a sign that read, "Don't mess with Texas!" A Texan told me that it meant, "don't litter the highways." So? Don't threaten me. Why not just say, "Texas loves you, please keep Texas clean?" Now before you get upset, beloved Texans, I want to make the point that my mother told me often, "You can't draw flies with vinegar." I know people who believe that if all the conditions they set for friendship are not met, they will not be your friends. Just relax! Fall apart! Chill, have fun. Life is too short to believe that you can expect everyone around you to meet all of your conditions and you will still have long-lasting relationships.

Rule 3

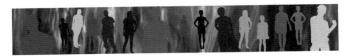

Forget it…. What difference does it make? You've got the world by the tail!

One of the greatest attributes that my mother possessed was the ability to minimize the effect that my mistakes had on my life. If she said it once, she said it ten thousand times, "Just forget it!" By dwelling on your mistakes and failures, you actually live in the past and cannot cultivate properly the relationships that you have in the present. Some people beat themselves up so much, we hate to see them coming. We know that all that they will talk about is their misfortune. Hey, forget it!

Rule 4

Ask your friend few favors.

A ccept a favor freely offered, but don't overdo it. When you always come around to ask favors, the relationship begins to be rooted in the favor and not in mutual love and respect. A good example of how too many favors can hurt a relationship is this. A friend comes to you regularly to ask your help with certain things, or to use your influence with someone that they need to do them a favor. After several affirmative responses on your part, you finally say, "No, I can't do that this time." What is your friend's response? "Well… thanks, but no thanks!" He is hurt and the relationship is practically over. Be careful asking too many favors.

Rule 5

Never borrow money from a friend.

G o to the bank to borrow money. The reason you go to a friend to get money is because you don't have any. You assume that you will have some later, but you may not. Have you ever loaned someone money and were not paid back? How do you feel about the little weasel? Yeah, me too! When you borrow money, there will always be that sense of indebtedness. Even when you pay it back your friend may feel that you owe him something. The habit of borrowing money from friends has divided many friendships.

Rule 6

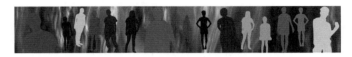

Invest time in your friends.

The value of the relationship will increase relative to the amount of time you invest in it. The more time I invest in my wife, the more valuable my marriage is to me. As with the stock market, your job, or a hobby, the more you invest in people the more they will mean to you and the more you will value them.

Rule 7

Let your subordinates shine.

If they shine bright enough, it will reflect on you. I have learned that the main responsibility I have in my relationships with the people who are my subordinates in the organization is to make each one look as good as I can. The better they look, the better I look. It is my quest then to empower, train, encourage and put them in the place where they can shine the most. Everybody wins!

Rule 8

Give the credit away.

If you are mature enough to let someone else get the credit for a victory or an accomplishment, you will have many victories in your life. Early in my work experience, I was employed at a large chemical plant. In my department I had to handle a piece of machinery that utilized a certain type of air valve that controlled the airflow to molten plastic. It never worked just right. So after many experiments, I designed a valve that worked great. I had not thought much more about it until some months later, we had a meeting of everyone on my shift. The department head was complimenting everyone on a job well done, then mentioned an award for the person that had redesigned the air valve for the hot melt extruder. I was amazed at what happened next. They called out my supervisor's name and gave him the award. I wasn't crushed, only a little disgusted with the man who stole the credit from me. That day I lost all respect for that supervisor and learned a great lesson. The man who takes credit away from someone else is a thief. Give it away and make many friends.

Rule 9

Listen long.

Someone said, "The reason we have one mouth and two ears is because we should listen twice as much as we talk." Great thought. Listening is an art. It is the ability to value what is being said, more than what you want to say. We learn when we listen. We appear intelligent, studious, and respectful. Be quiet and keep it that way! We rarely get in trouble listening and always get in trouble when we open our mouths. Encouraging words that bestow grace are always a blessing, but listen first and listen long. You would be amazed at what you can learn about a person when you listen. Listen with your ears and listen with your eyes. Body language often says more than the tongue. Become a student of listening. Practice it twice as much as talking. People will seek you out to befriend you.

Rule 10

Don't make promises.

My dear pastor, Brother Roy, when asked for a commitment to something, would always say, "We'll see." It kept him from having to make a lot of commitments he was not ready to make, and it left the people he said that to with the proper expectations. My mother would often say, "I'll try." If she was not able to pull off what I expected her to do, all I could say was, "Well, she tried!" I have been let down a thousand times by good people who are long on promises and short on fulfillment. I still love them, but don't have any confidence in their word. As a result, my desire to spend time with them has diminished. Sad but true, a person that does not keep his/her word loses my respect and yours too.

Rule 11

Keep your word; do what you say.

G reat is the person whose word is their bond. Nothing is more refreshing than to be able to count on someone's word. Few people that I know consistently keep their word, all their word. We have become experts at worming out of commitments, backing out of promises, and conveniently forgetting what we said we would do. It has come to the point that when someone keeps his/her word, I will purpose to do business, develop a relationship and befriend him/her. It is so rare to find someone like that, that you want to hold on to him/her. Respect is owed to everyone, especially to the one that keeps his word.

Rule 12

Maintain equality in every relationship.

Blessed is the man that does not exalt himself over another. If on every occasion that you spend time with a friend, a boss, or an acquaintance they "pull rank" on you, you will tire of the relationship. There is no greater "turn off" than to have spent time with someone and leave feeling "brow-beaten." Pastors have to be careful in the pulpit not to preach down to their congregations, parents have to be aware of the danger of making their children feel inferior, bosses must be careful not to undermine the self-confidence and esteem of their employees. It is fatal to some relationships when one person holds a superior "plane" over the other. There should be no hierarchy, no true upper echelon. We are all just unprofitable servants; some have just done better in life.

Rule 13

Know when to change metaphors in your relationships.

Many parents still treat their adult children like they are mental juveniles. They have not recognized the maturity and adulthood that has been achieved by their child and the result is that the relationship breaks down.

As a father, I was the judge, a coach, the authority, a teacher, and a friend to my children. I had to be sensitive to exactly what metaphor was required of me in a given situation. If, when they came to me, I were always the judge, they would have avoided me. Think of how frustrated you would be if, every time you went to your friend or father, they would instruct you on "how it should be done." Ignoring your friendship, overlooking the possibility that you just needed someone to talk to, they felt the urgency to teach you or correct you.

Some times it is necessary to just put down all of the roles and be a friend. My children deeply respected me and I respected them. They would readily obey me when I spoke. They would never speak harshly or disrespect my wife or me. However, there were "friend times" when they could call me silly names, punch on me, and get away with "murder."

Once, when I was the pastor of a local church and principal of a Christian school, I was playing basketball with some of the students. One particular student named Eric was highly competitive and given to outbursts of emotion. During the game, I chose the wrong metaphor and taunted Eric like a competitor instead of encouraging him like a mentor. Eventually he got mad and threw the ball at me hitting me quite hard. I grimaced at the impact of the ball, threw it back to him and kept playing without saying a word to him. The next day at school he came into my office nearly in tears. I will never forget what he said to me: "Brother Billy, I am sorry that I threw the ball at you yesterday, and I want to thank you for not chewing me out in front of all of my friends. You are my pastor and my principal and I was wrong to do that."

Though both of us were wrong, grace redeemed the situation – a lesson I will never forget.

Rule 14

Never violate the confidence of a friend or an adversary.

You know that you have reached the pinnacle of a relationship when that person shares his/her secrets with you. When this occurs you must keep their words secret. To possess the confidence of another person is a sacred trust. My wife is the confidant in my life that I share my secrets with. She would never repeat them. This way I am accountable to her and she to me. Even your adversaries will respect you when you keep the things they tell you in confidence. One habit we should get into is to put every secret that a person reveals to us way on the back burner and for all practical purposes forget it. Don't bring it back up again to your friend unless he does. You will become a valuable friend when you are a "keeper of a trust."

Rule 15

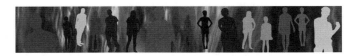

Only speak negatively of ideas and actions, not people.

Even in close friendships there can be opposing views on many issues. To let an opposing view on an idea come between friends is a mistake. Never let the differences of opinions become personal attacks on one another. We might root for different teams, prefer opposing candidates or even act differently in a given situation. Let the negativity stay in the arena of ideas and actions, protect the person. In marriage as in friendships, there will always be differences in tastes and preferences. Learn to appreciate each other's differences and let the relationship grow. What a person believes in his heart is what he is. So when disagreeing on ideas, be sure to respect that person's beliefs.

Rule 16

Avoid Anger

Anger begets anger. Most of the time, in my experience, anger is an immature response to a situation. When we allow anger to overcome us, we abandon our emotions to uncontrollable impulses. Anger leads to emotional attacks, insult and even physical harm. When you feel like anger is coming on, stop, break the cycle and begin to consider other responses.

Rule 17

Avoid angry people.

A ngry people are characterized by outbursts of criticism, violence and temper when things don't go their way. When someone causes them inconvenience, or disagrees with them, they have the tendency to explode emotionally, verbally, and often physically. When we consort with these kinds of people, we bring on ourselves the consequences of their outbursts and actions. There is no innocent bystander when we "hang" with angry people and they drag us into the fray of their actions. "He that passes by, and meddles with strife belonging not to him, is like one that takes a dog by the ears." (Proverbs 26:17 -KJV)

Rule 18

Don't expect too much from people.

Though we do and should expect some things from our friends and co-workers, it is a mistake to expect too much. When we have high expectations of someone, a friend, a child, a spouse or an employee, we are setting ourselves up for disappointment. High expectations are hardly ever achieved, and if the relationship is based on those expectations, it will suffer when the expectations are not met.

Rule 19

Never take advantage of a person's weakness.

I t is the proverbial "bully" that seeks out the weaknesses of people in order to gain something from them. This moves into the arena of Third World dictatorship where those in power exploit the helpless population. Pathetic is the person that has to depend on the weakness of the other person to gain the upper hand in a given situation. Needy, weak people need our protection and guidance. To violate their misguided trust, or take advantage of their inability to protect themselves, is to be led by "gutter instincts."

Rule 20

When you back someone in a corner, let him out.

Remember the story of Joseph, the favored son of Jacob. After having been sold into slavery by his big brothers, being thrown into prison, abused, falsely accused and forgotten for all of his young life, Joseph finds himself in the position to retaliate against them. Because of the famine, Joseph's brothers had to come to him to get grain. They didn't recognize him, but Joseph recognized them. He had them right where he wanted them and could have had them put to death. Instead, he used the situation to honor God and he let them go, blessing rather than punishing them. You will always gain when you forgive, release, exonerate, and let your adversary go free. You could make a friend for life when you let him escape certain loss by setting him free.

Rule 21

Don't criticize a person's children.

When you "touch" someone's child you touch his/her heart and soul. Every parent knows his/her child's weaknesses and strengths. They have learned how to cope with the behavior and problems their children may have and can see the whole child clearly where we only see their immediate actions. Every parent is given grace for their children from God, grace that you may not have for them. A parent will defend to the death their children and will most always be offended when someone speaks out against them. It may be okay to offer constructive advice if you are very close to the family. But it's best to wait until you've been asked.

Rule 22

Avoid being too competitive in things that really matter. You may win the battle and lose the war.

You may win the contest and lose the relationship. Let's face it, whether or not you win the weekend golf game is not a life or death issue. You can go all-out in a tennis game and defeat them in a chess match. Your relationship will survive the contest. However, if the contest is over the affection of a child, demanding your way in the settlement of a family estate or wrestling for the upper hand in a marriage dispute, though you win, you may just lose. There is a time in our lives when being the winner could be devastating to the others involved. I have seen life-long fights ensue after divorce cases where one or the other feels they were treated unfairly, where relatives feel they were cheated in the distribution of their loved one's estate; or, during life issues, instead of giving in, they moved into the competition mode to their own detriment.

Rule 23

Only lead people where you have been or are willing to go.

N ever lead someone into the unknown if you haven't been there and don't know first hand what the consequences may be. Uncharted waters have their share of dangers and must first be explored. It is too common for inept leaders to send their subordinates into situations that could cost them dearly only to use them as test dummies to see if it is safe for themselves. It is cowardly. Be sure that the best interests of those whose welfare you have control over are protected from, not exposed to, unnecessary danger.

Rule 24

Never "milk" a friend for information.

Most people will give you the information that they feel comfortable with you knowing. If they want you to know more, they will tell you. When you insist that they give you more information by badgering them, they begin to feel "on the spot" and may share things with you that they really didn't want you to know. Often the information is confidential and making your friend feel obligated to tell you violates the confidence of the third party. When information is forced from someone, it hurts the relationship. I would avoid the person who always demands information from me that I did not want them to know. Most people would avoid such a person too.

Rule 25

Never use information that someone gives you freely, or in confidence, against that person.

That juicy piece of news that you just heard from your friend may get you to licking your chops… better just drop it! You never know when that person may need to have you as a friend, someone that they can trust. Confidence may be the building blocks for a new friendship. Who knows, you may need that person to cooperate with you in a situation that might meet a special need in your life or someone that you love. You may not know all the people that he knows and how he will speak of you after you have revealed his secrets to others. It is best to hold that information and keep it to yourself.

Rule 26

Say, "Thank you," often.

How sweet those two little words are to the ears of another person, and how obviously absent they are when withheld. A general attitude of "un-thankfulness" permeates our society. People demand and expect, and when they receive, take it for granted, believing that no one deserves the slightest acknowledgement for the service they rendered or the gift they gave. But how beautiful it is to hear the thankful chimes of a grateful heart.

Rule 27

Never conspire with others against a friend.

I n the end, it is a sickening feeling to realize that you teamed up against someone that looked to you as a friend. Even when the person is wrong about something they said or did, when you join sides against them you destroy any possibility that they would ever trust you again. It is better to dissuade others from attacking a friend, even when he has done something wrong, than to be guilty of "piling on" against him.

Rule 28

Don't walk too far ahead of your friend and don't walk too fast.

To wait up for them is better than to run off from them. It is a courtesy to take your time and walk in sync with others when you are out and about with them. It says to them, "I want to be with you." When we out-pace them and leave them behind, we are telling them, "What I am doing is more important than being with you." People are sensitive to "proximity" and want to feel that they are important to you, even more important than the ball game that you are walking to or the task at hand. I visited a missionary once that left me in his tracks everywhere we went. He would run ahead everywhere we would go. I was left trying to keep up with him and lost him in the hustle on a couple of occasions. It made the visit unpleasant and made me less eager to go back to see him.

Rule 29

Never let friends get blindsided by their obvious weaknesses.

As a friend, it is our duty to protect them from the certain harm that they will be subject to because of a weakness or because of not knowing the consequences of a situation. Also, it is not necessary to lie about a person's performance just to maintain the relationship. Tell them the truth and they can improve.

Rule 30

Don't offer advice without giving a disclaimer.

"This may not work, but have you tried…?" Sometimes a friend might mistake an opinion or suggestion as advice or counsel. If they try what you say and it fails it could hurt the relationship. A friend of mine had an investment broker give him a tip on a stock that he thought would really make him some money. The company went bankrupt and my friend lost all of the money that he had invested. To make matters worse, he was related to the broker. He swears to this day that the broker almost "guaranteed" it was a dead ringer for success. Had the broker said, "This is a very risky situation, but it has a chance of making some real money." The fact that the disclaimer was provided gives the relationship a second chance. You may choose never to listen to your friend's advice again, but at least you took it at you own risk and can't blame the other fellow.

Rule 31

Respect is not earned; it is owed.

Traveling around the nation and many parts of the world is just a fact of my occupation. As a result, I meet hundreds of people each year with whom I need to develop instant rapport. The temptation that I face is to be a little skeptical of them until I have had a chance to test their honesty. For me, this is not an option. The days I spend in each city or nation are very short and I do not have time to test the sincerity of every person. My choice is to "respect" them. I limit my involvement or commitment to them and I guard myself from entering into instant agreements on important matters, but I express a deep respect for the person, his/her work and family. This has given me the rapport that I need to be effective while I am visiting and builds a foundation for further cooperation in the future. On the other hand, if I expect them to earn my respect, I may never have the possibility to be sincere in my dealings with them. They will discern this and we may never get the needed rapport established to begin a lasting friendship.

Rule 32

Add value to every person that you have responsibility for or have a relationship with.

Without acting like a "know-it-all," learn to add value to people around you by giving instruction, hints, ideas, practical tips, insights, and skills training. Once, on a trip to Syracuse, N.Y., a friend of mine, who used to play golf professionally, and I went to a driving range to hit a bucket of golf balls. I was hacking balls all over the range and he said to me, "If you would keep your right leg straight and not let it bend, you will straighten out that slice." What a help! He was right; it helped me greatly with a very severe slice. Now, all I need to work on are iron shots, chipping and putting. Different people have spoken words into my life that have helped me be a better person, a better speaker, a better golfer and just better at life. The value that those words have added to my life is immeasurable.

Rule 33

Affirm and encourage people.

A ffirmation is the act of supporting and encouraging the efforts, gifts, self worth, values and goals of the person that you are in relationship with. Look for the positive qualities of each person that you relate to and help them see these characteristics as strengths that they possess. Most gifts that people have are clearly visible to those around them. Learn to be an agent to help others discover those gifts and employ them to improve their life circumstances.

In life there are always reasons to focus on all that is wrong, but there are many blessings to be discovered as well. People face incredible obstacles that can, many times, be obliterated with a word of encouragement. "Hey, don't let this bother you, you'll be fine." Or, "This is temporary, you are a winner and will overcome these obstacles." How about, "I know that you've got what it takes to be successful in this situation." Show a person the bright side of life and the situation that they are going through. Remind them that the lessons that they will learn will be an education that will help them in other areas of their life. Don't let them get bogged down in the present hard times. Lift them up with words of courage.

Rule 34

Help people improve in several areas of their lives.

As wonderful as words of encouragement are, nothing will take the place of helping people improve in the situation that they face. My middle daughter was struggling with algebra and needed the course to graduate from high school. No matter how many times I told her, "You can do it," without practical help to improve her skills she might never have finished the course. So, I became her tutor. This applies to every vocation, sport, technical skills and even relational skills. Be prepared to help people improve their skills in order to be successful.

Rule 35

Don't hold back truth.

Truth, though sometimes hard to face, is liberating. Once the truth has been established in a given situation, all parties involved can discover the right thing to do. However, when you go along in life never really knowing the truth about your circumstances or what is interfering with a relationship, you will never resolve the difficulties. When conflicts go unresolved because truth is veiled, there is never the sense of closure. When truth is manipulated or finessed, you have non-truth… false assumptions. By allowing someone to believe the wrong thing about something you said or allow misunderstanding to remain un-corrected, you set the stage for the propagation of false assumptions. Clear up every issue with truth and you will have peace in your life and in the relationship.

Rule 36

Laugh at yourself, laugh with your friend.

L earn to be secure enough in yourself to laugh at your shortcomings. To try to hide your faults and mistakes is a grave error in relationships. It is ironic, but everyone knows when you are wrong, and they know that you know you are wrong, and often wait for you to realize it. If your friend is wrong or does something embarrassing, it is your responsibility to downplay the significance of the foul-up and when he laughs at himself, laugh with him. Some of the angriest moments of my life have been when people have laughed at me when I blundered or made a mistake. When others "rub in" your shortcomings you discover the shortest path to hate.

Rule 37

Never set up a friend for failure or embarrassment.

"With a friend like that, who needs enemies?" Ever hear that one? When you set up a friend to be embarrassed or to fail at something, in reality you act as their enemy. Never allow a friend, colleague, relative or anyone else to walk into a situation where they will get "whacked" if you have the power to stop them or the situation. Now, like you, I know people who are prone to do stupid things and get into embarrassing situations. Help them when you can, console them when you can't.

Rule 38

Never try to get sympathy.

One of the greatest qualities my father possessed was his refusal to ride on the sympathy of others. The reason I believe that this is an important quality is because I know people who play on the sympathy of others, and they come across so manipulative and insincere that I have lost my regard for them. Daddy was stricken with heart attacks at the age of forty and was disabled as a result of it for the rest of his life. He had several heart attacks over the remaining twenty-six years of his life and could have felt sorry for himself. He didn't, and he would not let us feel sorry for him. He worked as much as he could on the cattle farm that we owned and sometimes would collapse in the fields. We would rush him to the hospital where he would stay for a few days or few weeks. As soon as he got out, he would go back to the farm to pick up where he left off. As ill as he was, he never solicited sympathy. When people yearn for sympathy, they seem to build their lives around the negative instead of the positive. Empathy is a good replacement for sympathy, "I understand that what you are going through is difficult, but I am sure that you will triumph over the situation." This is much better than, "I feel so sorry for you, what can I do to make you feel better?" Please!

Rule 39

Be careful with practical jokes.

Practical jokes can cause harm, embarrassment and destroy relationships. What is even worse, it provokes revenge.

Rule 40

Don't allow a wealthy friend to always pick up the bill. Also, don't be cheap!

Know what a "mooch" is? A mooch is someone that expects everyone else to pay his way. Many of my friends are wealthy and love to treat me to dinner and lunch. That is great, but not every time. I will not allow them to pay for my meals every time we go out. A friend of mine had the habit of taking pastors from our church out to lunch often. He would always pay for their meals. At that time, I was also one of those pastors. One day, the second time we ate out together, I picked up the check and paid for it. He protested and said, "Let me pay for that!" I refused. He said, "That is my way of showing my appreciation for the pastors at the church. I take them out to eat and pay for it" Not with me. I make sure that I don't get into that trap. What if I begin to expect him to pay for everything and then he doesn't? It will hurt the relationship. Another story was shared by pastor/ author John Maxwell. John was at a convention with several other pastors from his denomination and after the convention many of them went to play a round of golf. Each pastor, when he went up to the club house asked the pro if he could get a discount since he was a pastor. The club pro gave them all discounts. When John walked up to the counter the pro asked him, "Are you a preacher too?" John answered, "No," and paid the regular fee. When he got to the first tee with the other pastors, they said, "John, you lied to that man about not being a preacher." John replied, "I'd rather be a liar than be cheap!"

Rule 41

Never flatter.

Want to butter me up? Forget it. Don't try to flatter genuine people; it goes against everything that they stand for. Flattery is nothing more than sweet talk! Sweet talk is what a man does with a woman when he wants favors. Even when I have accomplished something great, don't flatter me. Secretly, however, I love for people to say, "Hey, you did a great job on that." Sincere compliments are always welcomed and affirming, but flattery is insincere.

Rule 42

Get close, but keep your distance.

Don't meddle in people's personal affairs unless they ask, then do it cautiously. "Familiarity breeds contempt," someone once said, and it is true. You can stand by, offer help and even lend a hand, but some things are best left alone. There seems to always be some sacred things that even the best of friends don't want to share or have anyone else involved in. Learn what those things are and back off.

Rule 43

Honor the elderly.

On the underground tram at the Atlanta airport, there is a sign at the head of each car, "Please give up this seat for the elderly or handicapped." Does that offend you? It shouldn't. The elderly have paid an incredible price to preserve the society that we live in and to hold things together. The wisdom, grace and patience that they possess far exceed what we have to offer this world. The elderly are the Grand Sequoias of the human race. They tower over all of us in experience and knowledge and are wells of information for all who will listen. Give them your seat, give them your ear, and learn from the treasures of their insights and understanding. Sit down with a gray-haired man or woman and eavesdrop, you might learn the greatest lessons of your life.

Rule 44

Compliment a deed well done.

L ight up a face today. Tell the waitress that she did an excellent job and don't ignore the busboy. Tip the baggage handler at the airport a little extra and bring the flight attendants a box of candy to share. All of these gestures are ways to compliment the people that we expect to work extra hard for us, yet often overlook their exceptional service. Tell the colleagues at the office how much they mean to the success of the company, and the cleanup crew how much you appreciate a clean floor to walk on. You will make friends with some of the most important people in this world. Isn't it amazing that the most famous people in the world have as their closest friends, the maid, the cook, the chauffeur and the caddy? These people are the ones behind the scenes that make us look successful and should be acknowledged for the little, but hugely significant things they do.

Rule 45

Clean up after yourself.

I walked through the home of a relative once and saw the husband's clothes scattered from the bedroom door to the shower. I thought, "What a bum." I lost a little respect for him that day and learned a great lesson. If I do the same, people will think that I am a bum. I am getting better at this the older I get, and getting more aggravated with the people who don't have the training, intelligence, or enough consideration for others to clean up the mess that they leave behind. It only takes ten seconds, in most cases, to throw your clothes in the hamper, wipe down the lavatory, or clean up the dirt that you dragged in. So, do it!

Rule 46

Take the back seat.

Because I am the "guest speaker" at the places that I travel to, people always honor me with the "front seat." They say, "Billy, please sit up front." It is a blessing to get the seat of honor and I appreciate it. In the same way that I appreciate it, others do to. Many times when going somewhere with my friends I will climb in the back seat, (which is not easy for me) and let someone else get the preferred seating. It is a blessing to them and a way that I can show them honor. I like to single out the one that would least expect to get that seat. It means a lot to them. The hardest seat to give up is "first class" on an airline. Thousands of people travel constantly, as I do, and vie for the privilege of riding with the "eagles." I have named "coach" seating, "the coop." A coop is where chickens gather! So, it is even more difficult for me to ride with the "chickens" when I have earned the front cabin (this is a ongoing joke with my wife and me…I don't really believe they are chickens). The difference is nice meals compared to "chicken feed," and room to move compared to feeling like I am in a Spam can. Often, however, I have given my first class seat to the disabled, the weary, or a stern-faced wife when she expected that I would give her my seat.

Rule 47

Know what you are talking about before you say it.

Oh, the joy of listening to the person who is an expert at something that five minutes ago they knew nothing about! We would all love to be experts at something. The stock market, politics, computers, and marriage would all be subjects to excel in. The problem is that we don't have time to be experts in them all, so let's just be content to brag about our knowledge of peanut butter sandwiches and our favorite baseball team. I eagerly listen to people that talk about their job or their hobby, but can't bear to listen to the backseat quarterback who has never thrown a football, or the world traveler who gets all their information from The Travel Channel but has never left their state. Just stay within the parameters of your experience, first hand knowledge, training and exposure, and you will be a breath of fresh air to everyone that you talk to.

Rule 48

Avoiding acting like you "know it all."

Even though you may know more, you don't know everything. Confidence comes from study and experience, but there is always someone out there who knows more than you do. No matter how much you know there is always room to learn more. Every topic has a variety of related fields that explore more deeply the intricacies of the subject; and, more often than not, we should be learners rather than teachers. Acting like you know it all is a dead give away that you don't have a clue. So, be content with the information that you do have and be patient enough to gain more knowledge.

Rule 49

Forget all the past mistakes of your friend.

I t is easy to remind someone of their past blunders when you are angry with them. But all that this will do is add insult to the present injury. Forgetting is one of the greatest character traits that true friends have.

Rule 50

Be a "completer" not a competitor.

Helping others become better at what they do, greater at who they are and more complete in all aspects of their lives is our role as true friends. What does it matter if we are better at something than our friend if it doesn't help them become all they can be? Sometimes it is better to just let the other person rejoice at his/her accomplishment without reminding them that you did it better.

Rule 51

Don't blow your nose at the dinner table.

I t goes without saying that blowing your nose at the dinner table is repulsive… but I am saying it anyway. Many times I have been with people who just rear-back and let it blow without regard to others at the table. Friends may forgive you, but personal hygiene can affect how others feel about you. So, don't do it, it is a "turn-off" and inconsiderate of others, so take it out of the room.

Rule 52

Never pick your nose.

Ever catch yourself digging away at the little annoying crumb right in there, you know, in your nose? I bet lots of other people have caught you doing it too. For some reason it seems so natural but it is so demeaning. Just learn to take care of it in private places by appropriate methods. Don't get so relaxed around friends or family that you forget the little manners that you learned from your mom.

Rule 53

Clean the toilet after you use it… and the sink too!

On an airline flight from Germany to the U.S., I noticed a little sign in the tiny little restroom. It said, "Please wipe the sink and surroundings clean. Be considerate of other passengers." Now that is a novel idea, be considerate of others! I don't need to tell you how many toilets I see in airports, airplanes, and other public places that are needlessly filthy and unusable. I am not about to start cleaning up everybody else's mess, but I do clean up my own. Wouldn't it be great if everyone else did? This is especially important to do when you are with friends or at their homes. It seems like a small thing, but it says something about yourself to others. Be tidy!

Rule 54

Lend a helping hand.

Ever walk up to the door with bags filled with groceries? You look at your friend or relative watching the television, they glance up and see you struggling there… only it doesn't register in their mind that you could use some help. So, their eyes go back to the "Andy Griffith Show" while you attempt to open the door with your teeth. It is aggravating when the house needs to be picked up after a party night of family fun with friends and their children and no one else offers to pitch in to help you. You are reluctant to ever invite that crowd back over again. It is simple. When you see someone else start cleaning up the mess, pulling out or putting back chairs, or doing chores, lend a helping hand. You will be well thought of… and invited back as a dear friend.

Rule 55

Call if you are going to be late or if you can't come at all.

I t happens all of the time. We are sitting around with all the food on the table waiting for the last person to arrive. Only problem is, they aren't coming! And what is worse, they aren't telling anyone either. They could just pick up one of the three cellular phones on their hip, in the car, or in their hand and dial your number. But it is not gonna happen! It has happened in my life where a friendship ended with the inconsiderate "no show" person. Several couples were invited for dinner and one couple didn't show up. After the food was cold and the ice cream had melted, the rest of us ate. This couple never phoned us. After a few of these antics, I just stopped inviting them over. What a shame!

Rule 56

Call.

I f someone is truly a friend, call him/her. A short, "How are you," call means a lot to people. I try to make it a habit to stay in touch with friends. A call can help spark a get together and says, "I care," in a simple and effective way.

Rule 57

Admit it when you are wrong, everybody else knows it.

There is nothing wrong with being wrong. There is just too much to know anymore. I am the kind of person that likes to give out information when there is a discussion going on. I know that some of the information that I have is wrong and if I don't share it I will never find out. If you are wrong about something and you try to manipulate your "wrongness" to look like you are right, you will look like a fool. Just turn red, swallow big, and say, "I was wrong!" Good, now you've done it.

Rule 58

Don't discipline anyone else's child.

This is one of the great temptations of my life. Unruly and sassy kids really get on my nerves. Sometimes I would like to take the kids I see cutting-up and give them a thrashing. But, I'm not going to do it. If the parents are not going to correct them, then they will just have to live with the embarrassment of having undisciplined kids for the rest of their lives. And in the process, they will lose many close friends who cannot bear their children's lack of discipline.

Rule 59

Don't correct adults in front of others.

A s adults we do deserve to get some special treatment in the area of correction. It is too embarrassing to be corrected by one's peer in the presence of others. Don't do it. Respect people enough to take them aside and speak to them one on one. However, if someone ignores your correction and continues to act in an insulting manner (or pick their nose) you may have no other choice but to speak up publicly. Praise in public, criticize in private.

Rule 60

Don't lie.

To lie is to deny oneself respect. Those who lie make themselves a spectacle and in essence say, "I don't regard you enough to speak honestly with you." So be it, they don't deserve friends either.

Rule 61

Don't take it for granted that someone has agreed with you.

Ever happen to you? You thought you made it clear only to find out that the other party was just acknowledging what you were saying, but didn't necessarily agree with you. Always make sure that your friend is actually agreeing with you by letting them put into their own words what they are thinking. Otherwise, you will end up doubting the honesty of a friend when you took for granted something that wasn't so.

Rule 62

Never blame an innocent party.

God defends the innocent. When you blame an innocent party to hide your guilt, God Himself will take sides against you on behalf of the other person and you will ultimately lose.

Rule 63

Don't slam the door.

door slammed door can only mean two things, "I am mad," or "I don't care." Both can harm a relationship.

Rule 64

Don't laugh at another's calamity, only your own.

The emotion that should come into play at the calamity of a friend is that of compassion, not laughter. When you make fun of a person who has had a serious blow to his/her life, you give them cause to hate you. They shouldn't, but they would have cause. Be careful of how you treat a hurting person.

Rule 65

Never try to control another person's freedoms.

Y ou can give all the advice you want to, but you cannot control another person's life. As I raised my children, I let them make more and more of their own decisions. By the time they were in their mid and late teens, I let them make most of their own decisions. I raised leaders, not followers. I did not try to control their lives and I was never disappointed at the decisions they made. When we control the personal freedoms of another person we must take responsibility for all of their failures. The problem is that those who want control don't want responsibility.

Rule 66

Don't be legalistic; it is the root of gossip.

Legalism could be defined as "making rules for others that they cannot obey." The legalistic person sees everything that others are doing as wrong and criticizes them for it. It is possible that some of these things are wrong. But, by constantly making an issue out of it, those that hear your harping will begin to judge unfairly those who break the rules; and, this gives birth to gossip. "Did you see So-in-So do what they did?" The way the women in South Louisiana get away with gossip is to add, "Not to gossip, just to say!" Well…

Rule 67

Don't sweat the small stuff.

Major on the majors and minor on the minors. While eating lunch at my uncle's house one day I asked for another glass of milk. This infuriated my uncle and he threw his napkin down and stomped out of the room. I was only seven or eight years old and I thought, "What a big baby!" I never respected him again. Such a small thing made into a large offense. We do it all the time! Don't cry over spilt milk, or an extra glass of milk, life is too short to let the small stuff get our goat. Over-spending at the grocery store by five dollars, letting the parakeet out of its cage and it flies out of the house, spilling gravy on the carpet, your wife has a fender bender in the school parking lot…all minor infractions that should be simply forgiven and forgotten. Just drop it!

Rule 68

Sweat the small stuff.

On the other hand, sweat the small important stuff. It's the little thing that matters the most. The love note in the shaving kit when I am on a long trip, the call home, the surprise birthday party, the extra time spent with the middle child, your favorite dessert, and the little parting prayer on a long journey, these make the difference. Bring flowers to the home that you are invited to eat at, take a kid who has no dad at home with you on vacation, go out of your way to say "Hi!" to someone, and don't forget to say, "Thank you," "Forgive me," "I'm sorry," "You were right," "Excuse me," "I love you." These matter.

Rule 69

Don't take the biggest piece.

Love to eat? Love to eat a lot? Love to eat more than most? Yeah, I know all about it. It is hard to be polite when you have a voracious appetite like mine. However, occasionally I overcome appetite and give way to manners and just let the other guy have the biggest piece. I don't want to, I don't like to, but sometimes courtesy is more important than a full belly.

Rule 70

Never drink from the milk carton.

I learned not to drink out of the milk carton when I was a child. My daddy would go to the fridge and take a big gulp out of the milk carton. Do you think for a second that anyone else was going to drink after him? No way! To make sure, we would draw a skull and cross-bones on the milk carton that he drank out of, designating it as "poison" and "daddy's".

Rule 71

Don't forget to reward accomplishment.

We don't always do so great, but when we do isn't it a great feeling to be rewarded for it? It is. So don't forget when the wife cooks a great meal, when the daughter does good at the piano recital, and when a friend finishes college, make a big deal out of it, go overboard. Do something big-time to let them know that you noticed and they deserve a reward. "People don't want it, they don't desire it, they crave it!" Dr. William James.

Rule 72

Praise character.

I n a world of talented people with great gifts and no character, it is time that we single out the real champions, people with character. Look for people who are faithful, attentive, on time, flexible, honest, truthful, people who are caring, loving, humble, and polite. These are the giants of our day, praise their character not just their gifts and accomplishments.

Rule 73

Appreciate a pregnant woman.

With the disregard that society gives to the unborn these days, it is our job to make a pregnant woman know that we appreciate childbearing women and respect any couple that wants to have more children in their home. So many people look down on couples with large families and especially the pregnant mother-to-be...let's congratulate them and honor them.

Rule 74

Don't put a price of life issues.

Health, happiness, children, marriage, salvation... Sad will be the day when monetary issues dictate life issues. When the elderly are considered too old and unproductive to deserve quality health care, when we stop having children only because we can't afford them (of course, the new car is a necessity), and when budgets for world missions in our churches dry up. People don't marry today because they don't have enough money to live a certain life-style; marriages break down over financial matters more than any other issue. Is money so important that love is shut out when the checkbook can't deliver anymore? We should spare no expense to allow people to grow and live for the span that God put them on earth for. Then, when He is finished with us, He can take us home. Until then we should not put a price on the issues of life.

Rule 75

Don't ask a fat person if they have lost weight…. They haven't.

F or most overweight people their size is a bit of an embarrassment. They don't want attention given to their "fatness." When you ask them if they have lost weight, it brings attention to their size. Don't do it. Clothes can sometimes make a person look heavier or lighter, but chances are their weight has not really changed. So, no matter how much you would like to see your friend lose weight, just overlook their size and focus on some positive aspects of who they are.

Rule 76

Revisit the reasons that you became friends.

While looking at my high school annual, I came upon some old pictures of my wife and a note that she wrote to me. For a moment I had that "old-time feeling" and remembered how totally smitten I was when we first fell in love. It felt good. For some time I strolled down memory lane and recounted all of the wonderful things we did together and recalled many of the reasons that I fell for her to begin with. It was a great journey. I love her much more today, but will never forget what attracted me to her at first. When we revisit the reasons we fell in love or became friends, it helps strengthen our relationship.

Rule 77

Never call someone a "loser."

I was listening one day to what was supposed to be a motivational tape. The man was speaking at a convention of a well-known networking company and he referred to people who didn't see things his way as "losers." He surmised that people who didn't want to make more money or people that had to "work forty hours per week" were never going to be anything. Of course, those who participated in his business network and wanted to make more money were the winners. It made me sick. I turned him off and left with a very sour taste in my mouth for that company. When we tell someone that they are a loser, we pronounce a curse on them that they may not be able to overcome. It is better to say, "I know that you are struggling right now, but you are going to make it." The truth is, I have known scores of people who got involved in these network-marketing businesses and nearly all of them have failed. Many of them went on to new things and were successful. Huh…looks like they were winners after all!

Rule 78

Never remind a friend about a favor that you did for them.

When we do a favor for someone it is sown as an act of love and friendship. There is no need to be acknowledged for it. If you keep reminding your friend of that favor, he will regret that he ever accepted it.

Rule 79

One man, one wife, one love through life... Memories are made of this.

There are many "nightmarish" memories when a marriage fails. All who have experienced divorce remember the bitterness, the pain and the regrets. Though we don't live in a perfect world, we should never accept splitting up as the norm. It is so refreshing to meet couples that have overcome the odds and difficult times in marriage. These couples have wonderful memories of battles fought and won and wonderful times together. So, work on it, it's worth it!

Rule 80

Don't tell someone that you will pray for him/her if you won't.

In my line of work, it is encouraging to know that there are people who take the time to pray for me. Sincere people who will intercede on my behalf are valuable associations that I don't take for granted. However, I know that there are some that mean well when they say they will pray for me but never do. Try not to do the same.

Rule 81

Return phone calls, letters and e-mails... promptly.

Electronic mail, cell phones, and all of the new technological advances in communications today allow us to be more efficient than ever before. We can get more done, stay in contact better and communicate with multitudes of people. So, why don't we? Many of my calls and e-mails go unreturned. There are numerous occasions when I left a voice mail that I am sure was erased without being responded to. I know that most people today screen every call and e-mail and only answer the ones that they want to answer. At least you could just send a one-liner acknowledging that you got their call or e-mail and when time allows you will try to be more thorough in your reply. I have been asked to get together with certain people through e-mail correspondences. I answered and gave a time that I would be available only to never receive a response. So much for that! We never got together.

Rule 82

Don't be easily offended and don't take it personally.

This is the proverbial "chip on the shoulder." Insecurity, anger, jealousy, envy, and pride are the culprits that cause us to be easily offended. Most offenses that come our way are unintentional and were never meant as a direct attack against us. When we are too sensitive because of the above emotions, we become an "offended person looking for a place to happen." Before you get your feelings hurt, ask yourself, "Am I sure that the person really meant to hurt me or attack me?" Chances are, they didn't. It is time to outgrow the "everybody is against me" attitude. Offenses are like bees. They buzz around and every now and then they might just land on your shoulder and give you a little sting. Shrug it off; don't let it become a heart attack! People are against you, they are just for themselves.

Rule 83

Never tell someone that they are ugly.

The only ugly person in the world is the person who had no mother! Since there are no people in the world who did not have a mother, there are no ugly people, at least in the eyes of the mothers. When we tell someone that they are "ugly," we curse them with a stigma that they can't change. They may live their lives feeling inferior to others in the area of outward features. The only "really ugly" people in this world are those who are ugly on the inside. And most of the time, these people appear beautiful on the outside, but can never live up to that beauty as a real person. Keep your opinions of others who are not blessed with outward beauty to yourself and you will never hurt them.

Rule 84

Don't overreact when criticized, some of it is probably true.

No one likes to be criticized! Criticism bothers us most when we think we have done a good job or at least our best. First look at the person who is doing the criticizing. Is their opinion or judgment credible? Do they fully understand what you are trying to accomplish? If so, listen to them and thank them for the "help." If not, smile and go about your business. Some people critique, others criticize. Listen to both and ask yourself if it might be true. If it is true, then you have learned something about yourself and can make a positive change and improve. If it is not true, then forget it, you've learned something about that person. The best way to avoid the discomfort of criticism is to invite criticism. Then you will take it as a positive way for self-improvement.

Rule 85

Friendships cannot survive lies or prejudice.

Three sure ways to destroy a friendship is to lie to, or about a friend, pre-judge them because of their race, religion or past, and repeat a secret that they have shared with you. True friendships are built upon truth, acceptance and trust. To violate any of these is to undermine the support structure of that friendship. The greatest friend you will ever have is one who is trustworthy. You trust them that they won't repeat what you say, and trust that you are accepted by them just as you are. When friendship is built upon these blocks, nothing can tear it down.

Rule 86

Never curse – absolutely never curse a friend.

I t was always my opinion that people who cursed were ignorant. At least that's what it sounded like. I figured that the reason that they cursed was they didn't know what else to say or they didn't have the vocabulary to say it. If they would just take the time to think about it, maybe they could think of some other words that could be substituted for the "tip of the tongue" expletive. It really irks me to hear people curse. It immediately lowers my opinion of them, no matter what their position is. I just think less of a person after I hear them let loose a few foul words. As bad as cursing is, it is magnified when it is directed towards a friend. When one friend curses another, you destroy the sense of love and acceptance that was there. "If that is how you really feel, then this friendship is over." This is probably the kind of response you will get when you curse a friend. Watch what you say, "the tongue is a fire," and sets aflame animosity and hurt that can destroy a friend.

Rule 87

Rejoice at the success of your friend.

I can still remember the house trailer in the middle of the swamp where my friend used to live. He was a hard-working man with a big family and it cost a lot to live. He just didn't have a lot. Over the years I watched him struggle financially, but he remained one of my best friends. Then he discovered a business that he enjoyed and with his good work ethic began to prosper. Year after year he grew the business until it became very successful and made him a wealthy man. He recently sold the business for several million dollars and is semi-retired. I will never forget when my wife and I drove up to their new, sprawling home. It was beautiful. We were so excited for them. They had worked so hard and had come a long way. It is a long way from the swamp to this house on the hill. The feeling in my heart for them was thankfulness and joy. This is a feeling that I will never forget. I am sure that it made my friends happy to see me rejoice at their success, but not nearly as happy as it made me feel.

Rule 88

Grieve with those who grieve.

One of the most moving and comforting things that ever happened to me occurred at the funeral of my grandson. My family and I had gone through one of the most heart-breaking times of our lives. We were stunned and almost numb from the experience of watching our precious little one suffer and eventually die. We loved him so much, and now it was time to say good-bye, forever. I was so hurt by it all, but in the midst of it found comfort when my pastor came in, viewed the child, came and sat next to me and began to weep. I knew that he understood.

Rule 89

Don't make your friends always have to wait on you.

Tardiness is a habit. If you are naturally slow moving, get started earlier, but be on time. It can be aggravating to others to have to constantly hold up plans while you make them wait.

Rule 90

Stand up when someone walks in the room.

This is a simple act of respect that has been forgotten. At least stand up the first time you see that person that day. The response is normally, "You don't have to stand up for me." But you make a lasting impression of humility and respect when you do.

Rule 91

Avoid waking up on the wrong side of the bed; keep your bad mood to yourself.

Others should not have to pay for your miserable mood. I know a lot of moody people whom you have to walk on eggshells around when they are in a bad mood. Why make others feel uneasy just because things are not going well with you that day. Try to stay up beat and positive, or you will repel friends.

Rule 92

Never wake up in the wrong bed.

This is a no-brainer. When you are unfaithful to your spouse, you set in motion the wheels of guilt and infidelity that have a subtle, and sometimes not so subtle, effect on your relationship. Guilt sows seeds for lies and cover-up. You will end up always avoiding the truth to cover up the past. Then, if the truth is discovered ...it is the end of trust, which is one of the key components of lasting relationships.

Rule 93

It ain't yours...don't take it.

Leave things that are not yours alone. Do not desire them and do not take them. Stealing is unforgivable in a relationship. Even though you could be forgiven for stealing, you might never be forgiven for violating the trust issues in the relationship. However, if the person you stole from is a big enough person, you may even get another chance at trust, but it is not worth the risk.

Rule 94

Be yourself.

What good is it to try to build relationships around the person whom you are not or ever could be? Improve on who you are, because we all could stand a little improvement in our character and attitude. Then just be who you are. When people start liking you for who you are, you will feel good about yourself and won't have to pretend being what you were never meant to be. Being yourself around your friends makes you reliable and appreciated for the qualities that God created you with.

Rule 95

Forgive.

How many times in my life have I needed a friend or my wife to forgive me? I cannot begin to count how many. Nothing brings healing to hurts in relationship faster and more completely than forgiveness. I went to the home of a couple, acquaintances of mine, who had been in a "plate throwing, glass breaking" fight. When I got there, the wife was locked in the bedroom and would not come out. She was so angry at her husband for something that he had (supposedly) done, that she did not want to be reconciled to him…at that moment. I asked her to pick up the phone and said these simple words, "Until you forgive, this matter can not be solved." She came out, she forgave, and I left them hugging and apologizing to one another.

In forgiveness there is the power of healing and an opportunity for another chance… whether it be "chance" number seven or number seventy.

Rule 96

Don't worry about what people think of you; it is more likely they are thinking only about themselves.

Often, we sit around wondering what others might be thinking in their hearts about us. If we made a mistake or said something out of place, we think that their thoughts are only on our blunders. The fact is, however, that they are not thinking of you, they are thinking of themselves. Sure, sometimes a person is preoccupied with negative thoughts about you, but those kinds of people are thinking negatively of everybody. So, don't worry, their thoughts have no power over you anyway.

Rule 97

Preparation expedites timing.

W e are always waiting on God to call us. God is always waiting on us to get prepared. We are always waiting on relationships to get better; others are always waiting on us to get better in the relationship. Relationships will be better tomorrow if we would begin working on making them better... today.

Rule 98

Relationships help define your destiny.

Your identity is your destiny. The people you associate with and those that you are related to tell the world "who you are." Hang out with people of purpose, and you will be known as leader. Hang out with gang members and criminals and you will be known as the same. The people you relate to and associate with will undoubtedly influence your life in the direction that it goes and will determine whom you will become.

Rule 99

Never let the opinions of others define you.

If you let the opinions of others define you, you will never become all that God wants you to be. The people you know may not see the gift that you possess or God's design for your life. In time they should, and they will see who God has made you to be. So, in the meantime, improve on who you are and you will see the opinions of others line up with the real you.

Rule 100

Don't put conditions on happiness.

Avoid thinking, "Until this or that happens, I will never be happy." To be happy does not depend on reaching all of your goals in life; it is an attitude of gratefulness for where you have come from and for where you are now. When we defer happiness for some future time in our life, when we are rich, have the job that we want, or when certain relationships gel, we may never reach those milestones and may never be happy. Decide today that you are going be happy with circumstances the way they are now, with the people that surround you now, and with the place in life that you are now. Then you can pursue all avenues of success that will make you even happier.

Rule 101

Develop a good-self image.

Recognize that it is difficult to be a good friend if you think badly of yourself. You will only "be" what you really see yourself "as." When we think of ourselves as unlovable, rebellious, ugly, or unworthy to be someone's friend, it will nearly be impossible to live up to that friendship. However, when we see ourselves as worth being loved, an asset to the relationship, and important to the other person, we will probably be able to live up to that image. Though it is difficult to "remake" yourself, with God's help, you can be a greater person and friend than you ever thought possible.

THE LESSON FROM THIS BOOK

What you do for God will be measured by what you do for people.

How many stories have we heard of failed relationships that centered around the neglect of a spouse or family member in the name of "working for God"? Does not the work of God have as a primary focus the needs of people? Consider what the Apostle Paul said in II Corinthians 12:15, "And I will very gladly spend and be spent for you...." Christ, Himself gave it all for the redemption of people. Is there some institution, some cause, some higher calling that excludes people as its primary target? We serve God better by serving people better, we work for God more by working for people more, and we bless God by blessing people. Even our relationship with God is revealed in our relationship with people. "If a man says, I love God and hates his brother, he is a liar: for he that loves not his brother whom he has seen, how can he love God whom he has not seen?" (I John 4:20 -KJV) So, if you have a heart for God, to do His will and please Him, reach out to the people that Christ died for. "By this shall all men know that you are my disciples, if you have love one to another." (John 13:35 -KJV)

Other Titles by Billy Hornsby:

The Cell Driven Church
Realizing the Harvest

Success for the Second in Command

The Attractional Church

For copies of this book, please visit:
www.amazon.com

Association of Related Churches
1122 Edenton Street
Birmingham, AL 35242